AZERBAIJAN 2016 HUMAN RIGHTS REPORT

EXECUTIVE SUMMARY

The Azerbaijani constitution provides for a republic with a presidential form of government. Legislative authority is vested in the Milli Mejlis. The president dominated the executive, legislative, and judicial branches of government. On September 26, constitutional amendments were approved that, inter alia, increased the president's term in office from five to seven years and expanded the powers of the president. Other amendments included a provision permitting the further restriction of freedom of assembly. The constitutional referendum was marked by widespread credible complaints of irregularities. Legislative elections in November 2015 could not be fully assessed due to the absence of an Organization for Security and Cooperation in Europe (OSCE) election observation mission; independent observers alleged irregularities throughout the country. The 2013 presidential election did not meet a number of key OSCE standards for democratic elections.

Civilian authorities maintained effective control over the security forces.

Separatists, with Armenia's support, continued to control most of Nagorno-Karabakh and seven other Azerbaijani territories. The final status of Nagorno-Karabakh remained the subject of international mediation by the OSCE Minsk Group, cochaired by France, Russia, and the United States. There was an increase in violence along the Line of Contact and the Armenia-Azerbaijan border April 1-5. The heavy clashes led to the highest death toll since the signing of the 1994 cease-fire agreement. There were allegations of atrocities committed by the sides of the Nagorno-Karabakh conflict during an April 1-5 outbreak of violence. The sides in the conflict also submitted to the European Court of Human Rights complaints accusing each other of committing atrocities during this period.

The most significant human rights problems during the year included:

Increased government restrictions on fundamental freedoms: Authorities limited the freedoms of expression, assembly, and association through intimidation, incarceration on questionable charges, and harsh abuse of selected activists and secular and religious opposition figures. The operating space for activists and nongovernmental organizations (NGOs) remained severely constrained. There was a continuing crackdown on civil society, including intimidation, arrest, and conviction on charges widely considered politically motivated; criminal investigations into NGO activities; restrictive laws; and the freezing of bank accounts that rendered many groups unable to function. Authorities also restricted freedom of expression by closing a semi-independent television station that had been the country's sole independent broadcaster until late 2006, when its independence began to decline, and by taking actions that resulted in the end of the print edition of a leading opposition newspaper.

Government use of the judicial system to punish dissent: Authorities arbitrarily arrested and detained activists, engaged in politically motivated imprisonment, conducted trials that lacked due process, and subjected activists to lengthy pretrial detention with impunity. Authorities used different pretexts to decrease the number of defense lawyers willing and able to defend the rights of peaceful activists. While authorities released 17 individuals widely considered to be incarcerated for exercising their fundamental freedoms, they held an even larger number of others.

Government restrictions continued on the ability of citizens to choose their government in free and fair elections.

Other problems reported included physical abuse in the military; alleged torture and abuse of detainees, at times leading to death; police violence against peaceful citizens; abuse of inmates in prisons; harsh and sometimes life-threatening prison conditions; detentions without warrants; and incommunicado detention. Authorities often failed to provide due process, including with regard to property rights. There were reports of arbitrary government invasions of privacy, incarceration of religious figures, and restrictions on the religious freedom of some unregistered groups. Authorities restricted freedom of movement for a growing number of journalists and activists. Constraints on political participation persisted. While the government took continued measures towards reducing low-level corruption in government services, allegations of systemic corruption at all levels of government continued. Violence against women, gender-biased sex selection, and trafficking in persons were reported. Societal intolerance, violence, and discrimination based on sexual orientation and gender identity remained problems, as did societal stigma against persons with HIV/AIDS. Authorities did not effectively enforce laws prohibiting discrimination in employment or occupation.

The government did not prosecute or punish most officials who committed human rights abuses; impunity remained a problem.

Section 1. Respect for the Integrity of the Person, Including Freedom from:

a. Arbitrary Deprivation of Life and other Unlawful or Politically Motivated Killings

Separatists, with Armenia's support, continued to control most of Nagorno-Karabakh and seven other Azerbaijani territories. The final status of Nagorno-Karabakh remained the subject of international mediation by the OSCE Minsk Group, cochaired by France, Russia, and the United States. There was an increase in violence along the Line of Contact and Armenia-Azerbaijan international border April 1-5. The heavy clashes led to the highest death toll since the signing of the 1994 cease-fire agreement. There were allegations of atrocities committed by the sides of the Nagorno-Karabakh conflict during an April 1-5 outbreak of violence. The sides in the conflict also submitted to the European Court of Human Rights complaints accusing each other of committing atrocities during this period.

Both the government and human rights monitors reported a drop in harmful hazing practices in the military. As of November 20, local human rights organizations reported at least 36 noncombat-related deaths in security forces, including suicides and soldiers killed by fellow service members. On February 20, for example, another conscript shot and killed State Border Service (SBS) member Sanan Mehdizade. The SBS refused to comment on the death to media outlets. No further details were available.

b. Disappearance

There were no reports of politically motivated disappearances.

As of July 5, the State Committee on the Captive and Missing reported that 3,866 citizens were registered as missing persons because of the Nagorno-Karabakh conflict. The International Committee of the Red Cross (ICRC) processed cases of persons missing in connection with the Nagorno-Karabakh conflict and worked with the government to develop a consolidated list of missing persons. According to the ICRC, more than 4,496 persons remained unaccounted for because of the conflict.

The ICRC assisted prisoners of war and civilian internees and conducted regular visits throughout the year to ensure protection of prisoners under international humanitarian law. The ICRC regularly facilitated the exchange of messages between them and their families to help them re-establish and maintain contact.

c. Torture and Other Cruel, Inhuman, or Degrading Treatment or Punishment

While the constitution and criminal code prohibit such practices and provide for penalties for conviction of up to 10 years' imprisonment, credible allegations of torture and other abuse continued. In 2014, the most recent year for which data was available, domestic human rights monitors reported receiving 324 complaints of such abuse by security forces.

The UN Working Group on Arbitrary Detention reported receiving a large number of statements during its May 16-25 visit to the country from current and former juvenile, female, and male detainees it interviewed alleging that they had been subjected to torture and mistreatment. According to the working group, interviewees "described having a gun pointed at their head, severe beatings, sometimes lasting several hours, verbal abuse and psychological pressure, practices such as standing on one's knees for long hours, threats of physical and sexual abuse as well as threats to arrest family members."

Human rights defenders and media outlets reported at least four cases of torture or other physical abuse during the year that led to death. There was no single source to confirm the exact number of such cases. On April 27, for example, Sumgayit City police detained 37-year-old Rashad Mehdiyev, who died two days later, reportedly from abusive treatment at the police station. Police claimed Mehdiyev died due to a head injury incurred when he accidentally fell. Mehdiyev's family refuted the claims and released photographs of him with multiple bruises on his body, which they alleged indicated torture. There were no reports on the results of a subsequent investigation.

Reports from the UN Working Group on Arbitrary Detention and human rights activists indicated that most mistreatment took place while detainees were in police custody, where authorities reportedly used abusive methods to coerce confessions. In one prominent example, on August 12, police arrested N!DA youth activist Elgiz Gahraman for alleged drug possession after he disparaged a proposed constitutional change that would remove the age limit for presidential candidates. Gahraman was held incommunicado for six days at the Ministry of Internal Affairs' Organized Crime Department. Gahraman later stated that during his detention he was subjected to torture and forced to sign a confession.

In November 2015 law enforcement forces arrested a large group of religious individuals in Nardaran, including the head of the Muslim Unity Movement, Taleh

Baghirzada, on charges of alleged involvement in an effort to overthrow the government and put in place an Islamic state. During the trial of 17 of the individuals, Baghizada and 16 other Nardaran residents charged in the case informed the court they were tortured while police interrogated them at the Ministry of Internal Affairs' Organized Crime Department. The defendants specifically claimed that police officer Shahlar Jafarov beat detainee Farahim Bunyadov to death in custody and subjected them to physical abuse. Authorities did not investigate the claims.

Authorities reportedly maintained a de facto ban on independent forensic examinations of detainees who claimed mistreatment and delayed their access to an attorney, practices that made it easier for officers to mistreat detainees with impunity. For example, imprisoned Muslim Unity Movement leader Taleh Baghirzada and his lawyers stated that police tortured him for days in an attempt to force him to renounce his beliefs and provide false accusations against secular opposition leaders Dr. Jamil Hasanli and Ali Kerimli. The Ministry of Internal Affairs' Organized Crime Unit reportedly denied him access to his attorney for more than a month.

In another prominent case, imprisoned N!DA youth movement activists Bayram Mammadov and Giyas Ibrahimov stated during their trial that police subjected them to torture while in custody. The two youths claimed that officers beat them, forced them to disrobe, and threatened to rape them with truncheons and bottles if they did not confess to charges of drug possession after closed-circuit television footage showed them painting graffiti on a statue of former president Heydar Aliyev. Their attorney reportedly was only able to meet with them after they had signed the coerced drug possession confessions. Despite physical evidence of abuse displayed by Mammadov and Ibrahimov during the trial and appeals to the Prosecutor General's Office and Ombudsman's Office in Baku, authorities failed to investigate their allegations.

There were media reports of police violence against citizens not involved in political activity. For example, Bakhtiyar Ismayilov reported that police from the Barda Police Department detained and subjected him to inhumane treatment on the night of September 16 for mistakenly stopping a police car instead of a taxi. He showed numerous bodily injuries after allegedly being beaten at the police department and claimed that police employees warned him not to report the incident. After his public statements, media outlets reported additional allegations of abuse at the same police department from individuals who previously were afraid to speak.

According to official data, the Prison Service investigated 334 complaints against prison system officials for torture or mistreatment between 2009 and 2013. The Ministry of Internal Affairs received 984 such complaints between 2010 and 2013, and the Office of the Prosecutor General received 678 similar complaints between 2010 and 2013. According to the UN Committee against Torture, this was a strong indication that torture investigations were not conducted in a prompt, efficient, and impartial manner.

Although there were reports of a decrease in abusive hazing practices, local observers reported bullying and abuse in military units during the year. The Ministry of Defense set up a telephone hotline for soldiers to report incidents of mistreatment in order to hold unit commanders responsible, which reportedly resulted in improved conditions throughout the armed forces.

Prison and Detention Center Conditions

According to a reputable prison-monitoring organization, prison conditions were sometimes harsh and potentially life threatening due to overcrowding, inadequate nutrition, deficient heating and ventilation, and poor medical care. While the government continued to construct facilities, some Soviet-era facilities still in use did not meet international standards. Gobustan Prison, Prisons 3 and 14, and the penitentiary tuberculosis-treatment center reportedly had the worst conditions. Former prisoners and family members of imprisoned activists reported that prisoners often had to pay bribes to use toilets or shower rooms or to receive food. Detainees also complained of inhumane conditions in the crowded basement detention facilities of local courts where they awaited trial. They reported those facilities lacked ventilation and proper sanitary conditions.

Physical Conditions: Authorities held men and women together in pretrial detention facilities in separate blocks, but housed women in separate prison facilities after sentencing. Local NGO observers reported that female prisoners typically lived in better conditions than male prisoners, were monitored more frequently, and had greater access to training and other activities, but that women's prisoners suffered from many of the same problems as prisons for men. Human rights monitors reported four cases of children under the age of seven living in adult prison facilities with their incarcerated mothers. Convicted juvenile offenders may be held in juvenile institutions until they are 20.

During the year the Ministry of Justice reported 122 deaths in ministry facilities,

81 of which occurred in medical treatment facilities. The ministry reported the majority of death cases occurred from various illnesses including cancer, cardiovascular pathology, and tuberculosis. The Ministry of Internal Affairs reported one death by suicide in its detention facilities in 2016. According to the ministry, as a result of an internal investigation, two police officers were dismissed for neglect of their official duties and one person was subjected to disciplinary action.

Prisoners at times claimed they endured lengthy confinement periods without opportunity for physical exercise. They also reported instances of cramped, overcrowded conditions; inadequate ventilation; poor sanitary facilities; and insufficient access to medical care. Although the law permits detainees to receive daily packages of food to supplement the food officially provided, authorities at times reportedly restricted access of prisoners and detainees to family-provided food parcels. Some prisons and detention centers did not provide access to potable water.

Human rights advocates reported that guards punished prisoners with beatings or by holding them in isolation cells. Local and international monitors reported markedly poorer conditions at the maximum security Gobustan Prison.

Administration: While most prisoners reported that they could submit complaints to judicial authorities and the Ombudsman's Office without censorship, prison authorities regularly read prisoners' correspondence, and domestic NGOs reported some prisoners in high-security facilities experienced difficulty submitting complaints. While the Ombudsman's Office reported conducting systematic visits and investigations into complaints, NGOs reported that the office was insufficiently active in addressing prisoner complaints by, for example, failing to investigate allegations of torture by N!DA activists Bayram Mammadov and Giyas Ibrahimov.

Authorities at times limited visits by attorneys and family members, especially to prisoners widely considered to be incarcerated for political reasons.

Independent Monitoring: The government permitted some prison visits by international and local organizations, including the ICRC, the Council of Europe's Committee for the Prevention of Torture, the president of the Parliamentary Assembly of the Council of Europe, and parliamentarians and diplomats from European countries. Authorities generally permitted the ICRC access to prisoners of war and civilian internees held in connection with the Nagorno-Karabakh conflict as well as to detainees held in facilities under the authority of the Ministries of Justice, Internal Affairs, and the National Security Services.

A joint government-human rights community prison-monitoring group known as the Public Committee was allowed access to prisons without prior notification to the Penitentiary Service. On some occasions, however, other groups that reportedly gave prior notification experienced difficulty obtaining access.

d. Arbitrary Arrest or Detention

Although the law prohibits arbitrary arrest and detention, the government generally did not observe these prohibitions, and impunity remained a problem. On May 25, the UN Working Group on Arbitrary Arrests expressed concern about the conditions in the special facilities for persons with disabilities and over the ongoing prosecution of human rights defenders, journalists, and political opposition.

In one of the more prominent examples of arbitrary arrest during the year, according to activists, authorities detained 185 individuals prior to, during, and after authorized rallies held on September 11, 17, and 18 in opposition to the September 26 referendum on amending the constitution.

Role of the Police and Security Apparatus

The Ministry of Internal Affairs and the State Security Service are responsible for security within the country and report directly to the president. The Ministry of Internal Affairs oversees local police forces and maintains internal civil defense troops. In December 2015 the Ministry of National Security, which oversaw intelligence and counterintelligence activities and had a separate internal security force, was dissolved by presidential order. Its functions were split between the State Security Service, dealing with domestic matters, and the Foreign Intelligence Service, focused on foreign intelligence and counterintelligence issues. NGOs reported that both services detained individuals who exercised their rights to fundamental freedoms, including freedom of expression. The State Migration Service and the State Border Service are responsible for migration and border enforcement.

Police crowd-control tactics varied during the year. In some cases police detained peaceful protesters and used excessive force against them.

While security forces generally acted with impunity, the Ministry of Internal Affairs stated that in the first nine months of the year, it took administrative disciplinary action against 259 employees for violation of human rights and freedoms(197 cases), unjustified detentions (12 cases), and rude treatment (62 cases).

Corruption among law enforcement officers was a problem. Low wages contributed to police corruption. In the first nine months of the year, the Ministry of Internal Affairs reported it took disciplinary action against 16 employees in connection with eight cases of corruption, dismissing seven from their institutions, and reassigning nine others. It did not hold any of the employees criminally liable, however.

Arrest Procedures and Treatment of Detainees

The law provides that persons detained, arrested, or accused of a crime be accorded due process, including being advised immediately of their rights and the reason for their arrest. The government did not always respect these provisions.

According to the law, detainees are to be brought before a judge within 48 hours of arrest and the judge may issue a warrant placing the detainee in pretrial detention, place the detainee under house arrest, or release the detainee. The initial 48-hour arrest period may be extended to 96 hours under extenuating circumstances. During pretrial detention or house arrest, the Prosecutor General's Office is to complete its investigation. Pretrial detention is limited to three months but may be extended by a judge up to 18 months, depending on the alleged crime and the needs of the investigation. Authorities at times detained individuals for several days without warrants, and legal experts asserted that judges sometimes issued warrants after a person was detained. There were reports of detainees not being promptly informed of the charges against them.

On March 22, Sumgayit city police mistakenly detained Rashad Abbasov and used physical force against him until he falsely confessed to stabbing another person. Police later identified the true perpetrator of the crime and released Abbasov, who was immediately hospitalized due to numerous bodily injuries. Abbasov's family stated that police also used electric shock to force him to admit to the crime. Authorities did not investigate the mistreatment.

The law provides for access to a lawyer from the time of detention, but there were reports that authorities frequently denied lawyers' access to clients in both politically motivated and routine cases. Access to counsel was poor, particularly outside Baku. Although entitled to legal counsel by law, indigent detainees often did not have such access. In one case, attorneys for arrested youth activists Bayram Mammadov and Giyas Ibrahimov reported they were denied access to their clients for two days, from their May 10 detention until minutes before their May 12 trial. During this period police held the two activists incommunicado.

Police at times held politically sensitive and other suspects incommunicado for periods that ranged from several hours to several days. On August 18, for example, authorities detained opposition Popular Front Party (PFP) youth activist Fuad Ahmadli and held him incommunicado for approximately 10 days. In another notable example, in November 2015 law enforcement forces arrested a large group of religious individuals, including the head of the Muslim Unity Movement, Taleh Baghirzada, (see section 1.c.). Following Baghirzada's arrest, authorities detained more than 70 persons in different parts of the country. As of November 25, a working group of 24 activists considered 52 of those detained to have been arrested arbitrarily due to lack of evidence provided during court proceedings and were reviewing an additional 20 cases as possible arbitrary arrests.

Prisoners' family members reported that authorities occasionally restricted visits, especially to persons in pretrial detention, and withheld information about detainees. Days sometimes passed before families could obtain information about detained relatives. Authorities sometimes used family members as leverage to put pressure on individuals to turn themselves in to police or to stop them from reporting police abuse.

A formal bail system existed, but judges did not utilize it during the year.

Arbitrary Arrest: Authorities often made arrests based on spurious charges such as resisting police, illegal possession of drugs or weapons, tax evasion, illegal entrepreneurship, abuse of authority, or inciting public disorder. Local NGOs and international groups such as Amnesty International and Human Rights Watch criticized the government for arresting individuals exercising their fundamental rights and noted that authorities frequently fabricated the charges against them. In particular, police detained individuals who peacefully sought to exercise freedom of expression. For example, on November 7, police in Agstafa District detained PFP youth activist Vusal Zeynalov and charged him with resisting police. The local court sentenced Zeynalov to 30 days of administrative detention. The party headquarters reported that Zeynalov's critical posts on social networking sites prompted authorities to detain him.

<u>Pretrial Detention</u>: According to the Ministry of Justice, the prison population numbered 23,311 persons, including 730 women. Of these, 3,102 were in pretrial detention. Authorities held persons in pretrial detention for up to 18 months. The Prosecutor General's Office routinely extended the initial three-month pretrial detention period permitted by law in successive increments of several months until the government completed an investigation.

<u>Detainee's Ability to Challenge Lawfulness of Detention before a Court</u>: By law, persons arrested or detained, regardless of whether on criminal or other grounds, are entitled to challenge in court the legal basis or arbitrary nature of their detention and obtain prompt release and compensation if found to have been unlawfully detained.

<u>Amnesty</u>: On March 18, the president pardoned 148 prisoners. NGOs considered 14 to have been political prisoners, including Anar Mammadli, chairman of the Election Monitoring and Democracy Studies Center; N!DA activists Rashadat Akhundov, Rashad Hasanov, Mammad Azizov, and Omar Mammadov; journalists Hilal Mammadov and Parviz Hashimli; human rights activist Rasul Jafarov; and the deputy chairman of Musavat Party, Tofig Yagublu. Also released were activists Taleh Khasmammadov, Nemat Panahli, Yadigar Sadigov, and Siraj Karimov. There were reports that authorities pressed some of the released prisoners to write letters seeking forgiveness for past "mistakes" as a condition of their pardon. Several prisoners, such as the chair of the opposition REAL movement, Ilgar Mammadov, reported that authorities used physical abuse, placement into isolation cells, assaults by other prisoners, and threats to family members to extract such letters.

e. Denial of Fair Public Trial

Although the constitution provides for an independent judiciary, judges did not function independently of the executive branch. The judiciary remained largely corrupt and inefficient. Many verdicts were legally insupportable and largely unrelated to the evidence presented during the trial. Outcomes frequently appeared predetermined. Courts often failed to investigate allegations of torture and inhumane treatment of detainees in police custody.

The Ministry of Justice controlled the Judicial Legal Council. The council appoints a judicial selection committee (six judges, a prosecutor, a lawyer, a council representative, a Ministry of Justice representative, and a legal scholar) that administers the judicial selection examination and oversees the long-term judicial training and selection process.

Credible reports indicated that judges and prosecutors took instruction from the Presidential Administration and the Ministry of Justice, particularly in cases of interest to international observers. There were credible allegations that judges routinely accepted bribes.

Trial Procedures

The law provides for public trials except in cases involving state, commercial, or professional secrets or confidential, personal, or family matters. The law provides for: the presumption of innocence in criminal cases; the right to be informed promptly of charges; the right to free interpretation as necessary from the moment charged through all appeals; the right to review evidence, confront witnesses, and present evidence at trial; the right of indigent defendants to a court-approved attorney; the rights to adequate time and facilities to prepare a defense; the right not to be compelled to testify or confess guilt; and the right of both defendants and prosecutors to appeal. Authorities did not always respect these provisions.

Judges at times failed to read verdicts publicly or to give the reasoning behind their decisions, leaving defendants without knowledge of the reasoning behind the judgment. Judges also limited the defendant's right to speak. In the trial of Bayram Mammadov, for example, judges ordered Mammadov to stop speaking and left the chamber when Mammadov asserted his right to make a final statement.

The courts often limited independent observation of trials. Civil society activists and defendants asserted that authorities filled the courtroom with paid agents to occupy more seats. Information regarding trial times and locations was generally available, although there were some exceptions, particularly in the Baku Court of Grave Crimes.

Although the constitution prescribes equal status for prosecutors and defense attorneys, judges often favored prosecutors when assessing motions, oral statements, and evidence submitted by defense counsel, without regard to the merits of their respective arguments. Lawyers for the accused in the Nardaran case noted that judges and prosecutors left the courtroom together to discuss a defense motion before it was denied. Judges also reserved the right to remove defense lawyers in civil cases for "good cause." In criminal proceedings, judges may remove defense lawyers because of a conflict of interest, such as the placement of defense lawyers onto the witness list, or if a defendant requests a change of counsel.

The law limits representation in criminal cases to members of the country's government-influenced Collegium (bar association). The number of defense lawyers willing and able to accept sensitive cases reportedly declined during the year due to various measures taken by authorities, including by the Collegium's presidium, its managing body. Such measures included disbarment or threats of disbarment. For example, the Collegium disbarred lawyer Muzaffar Bakhishov after he criticized Supreme Court chairman Ramiz Rzayev. There were reports of Collegium pressure on lawyers. On April 1, the Collegium strongly reprimanded lawyers Bahruz Bayramov and Elchin Sadigov for "disrespect" when they objected to the court hearing the case of their client, Parviz Hashimli, in his absence. There were also reports of police physically intimidating lawyers, pressure from prosecutors and police, and occasional harassment of family members. Most of the country's human rights defense lawyers practiced in Baku, which made it difficult for people living outside of Baku to receive timely and quality legal service.

The constitution prohibits the use of illegally obtained evidence. Despite some defendants' claims that authorities obtained testimony through torture or abuse, courts did not dismiss cases based on claims of abuse, and there was no independent forensic investigator to substantiate allegations of abuse. Human rights monitors reported judges often ignored claims of police mistreatment. Examples during the year of judges ignoring such claims included the "Nardaran case" and the case against N!DA activists Bayram Mammadov and Giyas Ibrahimov (see section 1.c.). According to the UN Working Group on Arbitrary Detention, whereas it received "a large number of testimonies" of torture and mistreatment during its May visit to the country, none of the country's officials or detainees with whom the group met indicated that a judge had questioned a detainee on his/her treatment in custody.

Investigations often focused on obtaining confessions rather than gathering physical evidence against suspects. Serious crimes brought before the courts most often ended in conviction, since judges generally sought only a minimal level of proof and collaborated closely with prosecutors.

With the exception of the Baku Court of Grave Crimes, human rights advocates also reported courts often failed to provide interpreters despite the constitutional right of an accused person to interpretation. Courts are entitled to contract interpreters during hearings, with expenses covered by the state budget.

There were no verbatim transcripts of judicial proceedings. Although some of the newer courts in Baku made audio recordings of proceedings, courts did not record most court testimonies, oral arguments, and judicial decisions. Instead, the court recording officer generally decided the content of notes, which tended to be sparse.

The country has a military court system with civilian judges. The Military Court retains original jurisdiction over any case related to war or military service.

Political Prisoners and Detainees

In addition to the presidential pardons of 14 individuals widely considered political prisoners (see section 1.d.), authorities released three others in the spring: journalists Rauf Mirkadirov and Khadija Ismayilova, and defense lawyer Intigam Aliyev. Despite the release of these 17 individuals, local NGO activists estimated the number of political prisoners and detainees to range from 119 to 160. According to Human Rights Watch, at least 25 government critics remained incarcerated for politically motivated reasons at year's end. NGO lists included the following incarcerated individuals, many of whom Amnesty International considered prisoners of conscience (also see sections 1.f., 2.a., 2.c., 3, 4, and 5).

On June 28, the Baku Court of Grave Crimes sentenced Rufat Zahidov and Rovshan Zahidov to six years in prison on charges of alleged possession of illegal drugs. Human rights activists and their lawyer stated that both defendants were imprisoned for being relatives of exiled opposition journalist and former political prisoner Ganimat Zahid. Editor in chief of *Azadliq* newspaper Zahid resided in France and published articles critical of Azerbaijani authorities on his online news outlet, *Azerbaycan saati* (Azerbaijan hour).

On April 19, authorities allowed prominent activists Leyla and Arif Yunus to leave the country for medical treatment after a number of court appeals. In August 2015 the Baku Court of Grave Crimes sentenced Leyla Yunus to eight and one-half years in prison for fraud, tax evasion, illegal entrepreneurship, and forging official documents, and her husband, Arif Yunus, to seven years in prison for fraud.

On October 25, the Baku Court of Grave Crimes sentenced N!DA youth activist Giyas Ibrahimov to 10 years' imprisonment for alleged drug possession. Authorities had arrested him and fellow youth activist Bayram Mammadov in May, after closed-circuit television footage showed them defacing a monument of former president Heydar Aliyev with graffiti. NGOs reported that, while in custody, they were tortured into confessing to drug possession charges (see section 1.c.). On December 9, the Court of Grave Crimes sentenced Mammadov to 10 years on similar charges.

Individuals considered by activists to be political detainees included Muslim Unity Movement leader Taleh Baghirzada (see section 1.c. and the Department of State's *International Religious Freedom Report,* www.state.gov/religiousfreedomreport/) and deputy chairman of the opposition Popular Front party Fuad Gahramanli (see section 3). NGO lists also included individuals convicted in previous years, including REAL movement chair Ilgar Mammadov, who remained incarcerated despite a 2014 ruling by the European Court of Human Rights calling for his release; N!DA activist Ilkin Rustamzade; and journalist Seymur Hazi.

By law political prisoners are entitled to the same rights as other prisoners, although restrictions on them varied. Authorities provided international humanitarian organizations access to political prisoners.

Civil Judicial Procedures and Remedies

Citizens have the right to file lawsuits seeking damages for, or cessation of, human rights violations. The law does not provide for a jury trial in civil matters; a judge decides all civil cases. District courts have jurisdiction over civil matters in their first hearing; the Court of Appeals and then the Supreme Court address appeals. As with criminal trials, all citizens have the right to appeal to the European Court of Human Rights (ECHR) within six months of exhausting all domestic legal options, including an appeal to and ruling by the Supreme Court.

Citizens exercised the right to appeal local court rulings to the ECHR and brought claims of government violations of commitments under the European Convention on Human Rights. The government's compliance with ECHR decisions was mixed. For example, it implemented the part of one 2014 ECHR judgment requiring it to pay 22,000 euros ($24,200) in compensation to Ilgar Mammadov for violating his rights but failed to release Mammadov as stipulated by the judgment.

f. Arbitrary or Unlawful Interference with Privacy, Family, Home, or Correspondence

The law prohibits arbitrary invasions of privacy and monitoring of correspondence and other private communications. The government generally did not respect these legal prohibitions.

While the constitution allows for searches of residences only with a court order or in cases specifically provided for by law, authorities often conducted searches without warrants. It was widely reported that the State Security Service and the Ministry of Internal Affairs monitored telephone and internet communications, particularly those of foreigners, youth figures active online, some political and business figures, and persons engaged in international communication. There were indications the postal service monitored certain politically sensitive mail. For example, the postal service reportedly twice "lost" Popular Front deputy chairman Fuad Gahramanli's appeal of his case to the European Court of Human Rights.

Police continued to intimidate, harass, and sometimes arrest family members of suspected criminals, independent journalists, political opposition members and leaders, as well as employees and leaders of certain NGOs. For example, Elnur Seyidov, opposition Popular Front Party chairman Ali Kerimli's brother-in-law, remained incarcerated since 2012 on charges widely viewed as politically motivated. In February the Ministry of Internal Affairs of the Nakhchivan Autonomous Republic threatened to arrest the family members of exiled businessman Mammad Gurbanov if he did not stop criticizing authorities. Gurbanov left Nakhchivan after reportedly experiencing long-standing harassment and physical abuse by police.

There were several examples of the use of politically motivated incarceration of relatives as a means of pressuring exiles. In the summer of 2015, authorities arrested Rufat and Rovshan Zahidov, relatives of the exiled editor of the opposition newspaper *Azadliq,* Ganimat Zahidov. In November the two incarcerated relatives publicly denounced Ganimat Zahidov, but he had not been released as of year's end. In July 2015 authorities also incarcerated Nazim Aghabeyov, the brother-in-law of well-known journalist in exile Emin Milli. Aghabeyov was conditionally released on April 22. On September 29, opposition leader Jamil Hasanli's daughter, Gunel Hasanli, was released from prison after serving nine months on charges that activists considered were politically motivated.

In September, prior, during, and after rallies against the referendum on constitutional amendments, police interrogated and reportedly intimidated family members of political and human rights activists as well as of independent journalists.

There were also reports that authorities fired individuals from their jobs or had individuals fired in retaliation for the political or civic activities of family members.

NGOs reported that authorities did not respect the laws governing eminent domain and expropriation of property. Homeowners often received compensation well below market value for expropriated property and had little legal recourse. NGOs also reported that many citizens did not trust the court system and were therefore reluctant to pursue compensation claims.

Section 2. Respect for Civil Liberties, Including:

a. Freedom of Speech and Press

While the law provides for freedom of speech and press and specifically prohibits press censorship, the government habitually violated these rights. The government limited freedom of speech and media independence. Journalists faced intimidation and at times were beaten and imprisoned. NGOs considered at least six journalists and bloggers to be political prisoners or detainees as of year's end. During the year authorities continued pressure on media, journalists in exile, and their relatives.

<u>Freedom of Speech and Expression</u>: The constitution provides for freedom of speech, but the government continued to repress subjects considered politically sensitive. For example, in the period leading up to the September constitutional referendum, authorities arrested selected activists who criticized the referendum. Arrests included that of opposition activist and economist Natig Jafarli, the executive secretary of the opposition REAL Movement, on August 12. Activists who were arrested were secular democratic opposition figures, although authorities cited alleged ties to Muslim cleric Fethullah Gulen, who was accused by Turkey of having organized the failed July 15 coup attempt there, to justify some of the arrests. Activists whose arrests were based on such alleged ties included Fuad Ahmadli of the opposition Popular Front Party, and Faiq Amirov, the financial director of opposition newspaper *Azadliq*, who was also the assistant to Popular Front Party chair Ali Karimli.

In October Human Rights Watch reported the government continued to crack down on critics and dissenting voices, including through the politically motivated arrests of at least 20 political and youth activists during the year. The incarceration of persons who attempted to exercise freedom of speech raised concerns about authorities' use of the judicial system to punish dissent. In addition, the government attempted to impede criticism by threatening some peaceful activists who spoke out against politically motivated imprisonments--including those in the Nardaran case (see section 1.c.)--and by monitoring political and civil society meetings.

The constitution prohibits hate speech, defined as "propaganda provoking racial, national, religious and social discord and animosity." Under the September constitutional referendum, "hostility based on any other criteria" also is prohibited.

<u>Press and Media Freedoms</u>: A number of opposition and independent print and online media outlets expressed a wide variety of views on government policies. Newspaper circulation rates remained low, not surpassing 5,000 in most cases.

Beginning in 2014 the government blocked the sale of newspapers in the metro and on the street, limiting sales to government-approved kiosks. During the year the government restricted the sale of opposition newspapers at such kiosks. Credible reports indicated opposition newspapers were available outside Baku only in limited numbers due to the refusal of a number of distributors to carry them. In September the opposition newspaper *Azadlig* discontinued its print edition when it was unable to conduct banking operations following the arrest of its financial director, who was also an active member of the Popular Front Party. Authorities then prevented the newspaper from continuing payment on loans.

The law allows authorities to close media outlets deemed to be broadcasting extremist propaganda or discriminating on ethnic grounds, among other offenses. On July 29, the Baku Court of Appeals revoked the license of the semi-independent privately owned ANS television station based on a lawsuit filed by the National Television and Radio Council (NTRC). The lawsuit was initiated after ANS announced its intention to air an interview with exiled Turkish religious figure Fethullah Gulen and Turkish authorities protested the planned broadcast after accusing Gulen of plotting the July 15 coup attempt in Turkey. The NTRC accused ANS of propagating terrorism and violating the law. ANS appealed; on September 21, the Supreme Court upheld the Court of Appeals verdict, resulting in the closure of what had been the country's sole independent television station until late 2006, when its independence began to decline. It had operated for 25 years.

Foreign services, including Voice of America, Radio Free Europe/Radio Liberty (RFE/RL), and the BBC, remained prohibited from broadcasting on FM radio frequencies, although the Russian service Sputnik was allowed to broadcast news on a local radio network.

While authorities released six journalists and bloggers during the year, local NGOs considered at least seven journalists and bloggers and two writers/poets to be political prisoners or detainees as of year's end. For example, on January 29, the Absheron District Court sentenced opposition *Azadlig* newspaper journalist Seymur Hazi to five years in prison. Authorities continued exerting pressure on leading media rights organizations similar to that applied to other NGOs in the country.

During the year authorities continued pressure on independent media outlets outside the country and those associated with them in the country. For example, authorities continued the criminal case against Meydan TV initiated in August 2015. The Prosecutor General's Office investigated more than 15 individuals in the case for alleged illegal entrepreneurship, tax evasion, and abuse of power. Official pressure on journalists also included the incarceration of relatives of journalists in exile, including *Azadliq* editor in chief Ganimat Zahidov's nephew and cousin, and bans on an increasing number of journalists and some relatives of journalists in exile from traveling outside the country (see section 2.d.).

<u>Violence and Harassment</u>: Local observers reported 33 physical assaults on at least 21 journalists during the year. The attacks mainly targeted journalists from Radio Liberty, *Azadliq* and other newspapers, Meydan TV, and Obyektiv Television. For example, on November 26, police detained journalist Teymur Karimov from internet-based TV Kanal 13 after an unknown person attacked Karimov while he was preparing a video report on water supply problems in the Barda District. Police threatened the journalist with filing a criminal case on charges of assault if he did not erase all his recordings.

Impunity for assaults against journalists remained a problem. The Institute for Reporters' Freedom and Safety (IRFS) reported in August that more than nine out of every 10 cases of physical attacks on journalists remained unsolved. There were no indications authorities held police officers accountable for physical assaults on journalists in prior years.

Journalists and media rights leaders continued to call for full accountability for the August 2015 beating and death of journalist and IRFS chairman Rasim Aliyev, who reported receiving threatening messages three weeks earlier; the 2011 killing of journalist Rafiq Tagi, against whom Iranian cleric Grand Ayatollah Fazel Lankarani issued a fatwa; and the 2005 killing of independent editor and journalist Elmar Huseynov.

Lawsuits suspected of being politically motivated were used also to intimidate journalists and media outlets. During the year approximately 29 court cases were initiated against journalists or media outlets, with plaintiffs demanding 1.3 million manat ($720,000) in compensation; courts ultimately imposed 95,000 manat ($53,000) in fines.

The majority of independent and opposition newspapers remained in a precarious financial situation and experienced problems paying wages, taxes, and periodic court fines. Most relied on political parties, influential sponsors, or the State Media Fund for financing.

The government prohibited some state libraries from subscribing to opposition and independent newspapers, prevented state businesses from buying advertising in opposition newspapers, and put pressure on private businesses not to advertise in them. As a result, paid advertising was largely absent in opposition media. Political commentators noted these practices reduced the wages that opposition and independent outlets could pay to their journalists, which allowed progovernment outlets to hire away quality staff. In addition, international media monitoring reports indicated that intimidation by Ministry of Taxes authorities further limited the independence of media.

Censorship or Content Restrictions: Most media practiced self-censorship and avoided topics considered politically sensitive due to fear of government retaliation. The NTRC required that local, privately owned television and radio stations not rebroadcast complete news programs of foreign origin.

On June 12, police seized the work of the Ganun Publishing House in Baku under the pretext of having received a bomb threat to the building. Civil society activists reported that authorities raided the publishing house after it printed posters advocating the release of imprisoned head of the REAL democratic movement, Ilgar Mammadov. The director of the publishing house, Shahbaz Khuduoghlu, reported that police took some published materials and printing molds from the office.

Libel/Slander Laws: Libel is a criminal offense and covers written and verbal statements. The law provides for large fines and up to three years' imprisonment for persons convicted of libel. Conviction of defamation is punishable by fines ranging from 100 to 1,000 manat ($55.60 to $556) and imprisonment for six months to three years.

Internet Freedom

The websites of Voice of America, RFE/RL, and Germany-based opposition media outlet Meydan TV were intermittently blocked during the year.

Radio Liberty and the opposition newspaper *Azadlig* reported denial of access to their Internet-based resources on November 28 and December 2 for publicizing critical online articles on proposed legislative amendments in the parliament. These outages became chronic by mid-December, with Voice of America and RFE/RL becoming only sporadically available inside Azerbaijan. Although the government denied involvement, the outages originated from within Delta Telecom, a company with close ties to the government that controlled over 90 percent of Internet traffic in Azerbaijan. The government also required internet service providers to be licensed and have formal agreements with the Ministry of Communications and High Technologies. According to International Telecommunication Union statistics, approximately 77 percent of the country's population used the internet in 2015.

The law imposes criminal penalties for conviction of libel and insult on the internet. On November 29, the Milli Mejlis passed new articles to the criminal code that expand those penalties. Article 148-1, stipulates fines of from 1,000 to 1,500 manat ($556 to $833), or public works from 360 to 480 hours, or corrective work up to two years or one year imprisonment for insults and slander through using fake web nicknames or Internet profiles. A second new provision, Article 323, stipulates fines from 1,000 up to 1,500 manat ($556 to $833) or imprisonment up to three years for insulting the honor and dignity of the president.

There were strong indications that the government monitored the internet communications of democracy activists. For example, after detaining Popular Front deputy chairman Fuad Gahramanli in December 2015, authorities prosecuted him on charges related to his exercise of freedom of expression on Facebook (see section 1.e.). In addition, many youth activists who were questioned, detained, or jailed frequently had posted criticism of alleged government corruption and human rights abuses online. The activists included video blogger Husseyn Azizoghlu, who had posted videos online that mocked police officers for planting drugs and falsifying evidence and was detained for 15 days on January. Other cases involved Popular Front Party member Fizuli Huseynov, who received 30 days' detention on January 27 after having criticized the government on Facebook, and blogger Mehman Huseynov, who was briefly detained in September and threatened with physical abuse if he did not stop posting video and images of police violence.

The Freedom House annual *Freedom on the Net* report, covering the period June 2015 through May, stated that the government "demonstrated its willingness to shutdown connectivity in times of civil unrest, disconnecting the entire village of Nardaran from the internet for several days following police clashes." The report acknowledged that the government did not extensively block online content, while noting that "netizens" (citizens of the net) and their families faced arrest and intimidation.

Academic Freedom and Cultural Events

The government on occasion restricted academic freedom. Opposition party members continued to report difficulties finding jobs teaching at schools and universities. Authorities fired most known opposition party members teaching in state educational institutions in previous years. NGOs reported local executive authorities occasionally prevented the expression of minority cultures, for example, by prohibiting cultural events at local community centers and the teaching of local dialects.

b. Freedom of Peaceful Assembly and Association

Freedom of Assembly

While the law provides for freedom of assembly, the government severely restricted the right. Authorities at times responded to peaceful protests and assemblies by using force and detaining protesters.

While the constitution stipulates that groups may peacefully assemble after notifying the relevant government body in advance, the government continued to interpret this provision as a requirement for prior permission. Local authorities required all rallies to be preapproved and held at designated locations, often at inconvenient sites, although a site often used in the outskirts of Baku was easily accessible by metro and bus. Most political parties and NGOs found the requirements unacceptable and believed them to be unconstitutional. Authorities throughout the country routinely refused to acknowledge notifications of planned public rallies, thereby effectively denying the freedom to assemble.

As modified by the September 26 referendum, the constitution provides that public gatherings not disrupt "public order and public morals." The Venice

Commission's September 20 preliminary opinion on the proposed constitutional amendments noted that it is "almost inevitable" that peaceful gatherings may disrupt public order (for example, by disturbing traffic) or disturb someone's views on morality and yet be permissible under the European Convention on Human Rights. The commission concluded, "The State should allow such gatherings and even facilitate them provided that those disturbances are not excessive and help convey the message of the public event."

Early in the year, the devaluation of the local currency (manat) and worsening economic conditions sparked protests in different parts of the country, beginning on January 6 in the town of Saatli. On January 12, after dispersing a protest in Lankaran, police detained opposition Popular Front Party activist Nazim Hasanov and Musavat Party activist Imanverdi Aliyev. Both were sentenced to 30 days' detention on charges of inciting people to public disorder. On January 13, Interior Ministry security forces used tear gas to disperse protesters in Siyazan. Police later reported that 55 persons were detained for participation in the various protests.

Activists reported that police harassed and/or detained 185 persons before, during, and after authorized rallies on September 11, 17, and 18 against the referendum on constitutional amendments. The courts subsequently sentenced 12 opposition activists to administrative detention that ranged from eight to 30 days, allegedly for resisting police, and fined one opposition activist 200 manat ($111) for violating public order.

The law permits administrative detention for up to three months for misdemeanors and up to one month for resisting police. Punishment for those who fail to follow a court order (including failure to pay a fine) may include fines of 500 to 1,000 manat ($278 to $556) and punishment of up to one month of administrative detention.

Freedom of Association

The constitution provides for freedom of association, but the law places some restrictions on this right, and amendments enacted during 2014 severely constrained NGO activities. Citing these amended laws, authorities conducted numerous criminal investigations into the activities of independent organizations, froze bank accounts, and harassed local staff, including incarcerating and placing travel bans on some NGO leaders. Consequently, a number of NGOs were unable to operate.

A number of legal provisions allow the government to regulate the activities of political parties, religious groups, businesses, and NGOs, including requiring NGOs to register with the Ministry of Justice if they seek "legal personality" status. Although the law requires the government to act on NGO registration applications within 30 days of receipt (or within an additional 30 days, if further investigation is required), vague, onerous, and nontransparent registration procedures continued to result in long delays that limited citizens' right to associate. Other laws restrict freedom of association, for example, by requiring deputy heads of NGO branches to be citizens if the branch head is a foreigner. Authorities routinely rejected the registration applications of NGOs whose names contained the words "human rights," "democracy," "institute," and "society."

Laws affecting grants and donations imposed a de facto prohibition on NGOs receiving cash donations and made it nearly impossible for NGOs to receive anonymous donations or to solicit contributions from the public.

In 2014 the president approved a number of amendments to the administrative code and the laws on NGOs, grants, and registration of legal entities that imposed additional restrictions on NGO activities and closed several loopholes for the operations of unregistered, independent, and foreign organizations. The laws make unregistered and foreign NGOs vulnerable to involuntary dissolution, intimidated and dissuaded potential activists and donors from joining and supporting civil society organizations, and restricted their ability to provide grants to unregistered local groups or individual heads of such organizations.

A resolution detailing new grant registration implementing regulations, enacted by the Council of Ministers in June 2015, sets a 15-day limit for NGOs to register their grants with the appropriate ministry, 15 days for the ministry to approve or deny the registration, and an extension of 15 days if further investigation by the ministry is needed. Based on extensive authority provided in the 2014 amendments, the Ministry of Justice put into effect new rules on monitoring NGO activities in February. The rules empower the ministry to conduct intrusive inspections of NGOs, with few provisions protecting the rights of NGOs and the potential of harsh fines if they do not cooperate.

A far-reaching criminal investigation opened in 2014 into the activities of numerous domestic and international NGOs and local leadership continued during the year. The investigation covered prominent independent organizations focused on human rights and transparency in natural resource governance, as well as international organizations providing assistance to citizens. As a result of the investigation, at least 32 organizations closed rather than subject their staff to continued pressure and the prospect of incarceration. Authorities froze dozens of NGO bank accounts as well as the personal accounts of a number of organization heads. Domestic and international NGOs described the criminal investigations, arrests, bank account closures, and other pressure as a crackdown on civil society unprecedented for the country (see section 5). A few activists affiliated with the Extractive Industries Transparency Initiative (a civil society coalition) reported that the government lifted the freeze on their bank accounts. Others affiliated with the coalition reported government constraints on their ability to operate.

The government continued to implement rules pursuant to a law that requires foreign NGOs wishing to operate in the country to sign an agreement and register with the Ministry of Justice. Foreign NGOs wishing to register a branch in the country are required to demonstrate they support "the Azerbaijani people's national and cultural values" and commit not to be involved in religious and political propaganda. The decree does not specify any time limit for the registration procedure and effectively allows for unlimited discretion of the government to decide whether to register a foreign NGO. As of year's end, no foreign NGOs had been able to register under these rules.

The Ministry of Justice reported it registered 99 NGOs and did not observe the practice of nonacceptance of applications during the year. The Ministry of Justice registered the human rights-focused NGO of Oktay Gulaliyev immediately before the Extractive Industries Transparency Initiative board meeting in October, but it changed its name and removed all references to human rights. Some experts estimated 1,000 NGOs remained unregistered.

c. Freedom of Religion

See the Department of State's *International Religious Freedom Report* at www.state.gov/religiousfreedomreport/.

d. Freedom of Movement, Internally Displaced Persons, Protection of Refugees, and Stateless Persons

The law provides for freedom of internal movement, foreign travel, emigration, and repatriation, and the government generally respected these rights; however, the government limited freedom of movement for an increasing number of activists and journalists.

The government cooperated with the Office of the UN High Commissioner for Refugees (UNHCR) and other humanitarian organizations in providing protection and assistance to internally displaced persons (IDPs), refugees, returning refugees, asylum seekers, stateless persons, and other persons of concern.

<u>Foreign Travel</u>: The number of activists and journalists whom the authorities prevented from traveling outside the country increased compared to the previous year. Examples included Popular Front Party chairman Ali Kerimli (since 2006), blogger Mehman Huseynov, investigative journalist Khadija Ismayilova, lawyers Intigam Aliyev and Asabali Mustafayev, opposition REAL members Natig Jafarli and Azer Gasimli, Emin Milli's brother-in-law Nazim Agabeyov, and at least 15 freelance journalists who filed material with Meydan TV.

The law requires men of draft age to register with military authorities before traveling abroad. Authorities placed some travel restrictions on military personnel with access to national security information. Citizens charged with or convicted of criminal offenses but given suspended sentences were also not permitted to travel abroad.

Internally Displaced Persons

UNHCR reported 613,129 registered IDPs in the country as of December 31, including persons in IDP-like situations. The vast majority fled their homes between 1988 and 1993 as a result of the Nagorno-Karabakh conflict.

The IDPs were initially required to register their places of residence with authorities and could live only in approved areas. This "propiska" registration system, which formally ceased to exist after the breakup of the Soviet Union, was enforced mainly against persons who were forced from their homes after separatists, with Armenia's support, took control of Nagorno-Karabakh and seven surrounding Azerbaijani territories. The government asserted that registration was needed to keep track of IDPs to assist them.

According to the Internal Displacement Monitoring Center, many IDPs who resided in Baku were unable to register their residences or gain access to formal employment, government assistance, health care, education, or pensions and had difficulty buying property.

Significant numbers of IDPs remained in overcrowded collective centers, where they were socially marginalized with limited employment opportunities and high rates of poverty. The law requires IDPs to register in the districts where they reside, and registration is necessary to obtain IDP status. Temporary registration where IDPs reside does not restrict migration within the country.

According to the government, it allocated 290 million manat ($161 million) to the State Committee for IDPs during the year. UNHCR reported that during the year the government rehoused 1,620 families, representing approximately 7,000 individuals, primarily in Fizuli, Sabirabad, Baku, Gazakh, and Zagatala.

Protection of Refugees

Access to Asylum: The law provides for the granting of asylum or refugee status, and the government has established a system for providing protection to some refugees through the Refugee Status Determination Department at the State Migration Service, which is responsible for all refugee matters. Although UNHCR noted some improvements, the country's refugee-status determination system did not meet international standards. International NGOs continued to report that the service remained inefficient and did not operate transparently.

Safe Country of Origin/Transit: According to UNHCR, the country did not allow Russian citizens fleeing the conflict in Chechnya access to the national asylum procedure. UNHCR noted, however, that the country tolerated the presence of Chechen asylum seekers and accepted UNHCR's role in providing for their protection and humanitarian needs.

Access to Basic Services: The estimated 1,193 refugees in the country lacked access to social services.

Stateless Persons

Amendments to the constitution adopted by referendum on September 26 allow Azerbaijani citizenship to be removed "as provided by law." Previously, the constitution explicitly prohibited the loss of citizenship.

According to UNHCR statistics, there were 3,585 persons in the country under UNHCR's statelessness mandate at the end of the year. According to the State Migration Service, 245 foreigners and stateless persons were granted citizenship during the year, and citizenship was restored to two persons. The vast majority of stateless persons were ethnic Azeris from Georgia or Iran. NGOs stated there were many other undocumented stateless persons, with estimates ranging from hundreds to tens of thousands.

While the law provides for the right to apply for stateless status, some persons could not obtain the documentation required for the application and therefore remained formally unrecognized. The law on citizenship makes it difficult for foreigners and stateless persons to obtain citizenship.

For the most part, stateless persons enjoyed freedom of movement. The law permits stateless persons access to basic rights, such as access to health care and employment. Nevertheless, their lack of legal status at times hindered stateless persons' access to these rights.

Section 3. Freedom to Participate in the Political Process

Although the constitution provides citizens the ability to choose their government through free and fair elections based on universal and equal suffrage, held by secret ballot, the government continued to restrict this ability by interfering in the electoral process. While the law provides for an independent legislative branch, the Milli Mejlis exercised little initiative independent of the executive branch.

Elections and Political Participation

Recent Elections: The OSCE Office for Democratic Institutions and Human Rights (ODIHR) cancelled its observation of the November 2015 legislative elections when the government refused to accept ODIHR's recommended number of election observers. Without ODIHR participation, it was impossible to assess properly the fairness of the elections.

Independent local and international monitors who observed the election alleged a wide range of irregularities throughout the country, including blocking observers from entering polling stations, ballot stuffing, carousel voting, and voting by unregistered individuals; opposition monitors also alleged such irregularities. The country's main opposition parties boycotted the election.

The 2013 presidential election fell short of international standards. In their joint statement of preliminary findings and conclusions on the election, ODIHR and the OSCE Parliamentary Assembly highlighted serious shortcomings that needed to be addressed for the country to meet its OSCE commitments fully. On election day, OSCE Parliamentary Assembly and ODIHR observers noted procedural irregularities, including ballot box stuffing, serious problems with vote counting in

58 percent of observed polling stations, and failure to record the number of ballots received. The ODIHR report noted that, prior to election day, the government maintained a repressive political environment that did not provide the fundamental freedoms of assembly, association, and expression necessary for a free and fair electoral competition. Authorities interfered with the media and civil society routinely, sometimes violently interrupted peaceful rallies and meetings before and occasionally during the 23-day campaign period, and jailed a number of opposition and youth activists. Neither the election administration nor the judiciary provided effective redress for appeals. Credible NGOs reported similar shortcomings.

On September 26, the government conducted a referendum on 29 proposed constitutional amendments, with voters having the option to vote on each proposed amendment separately. Amendments included provisions extending the presidential term from five to seven years, permitting the president to call early elections if twice in one-year legislators pass no-confidence measures in the government or reject presidential nominees to key government posts. The amendments also authorized the president to appoint one or more vice presidents, designating the senior vice president as first in the line of presidential succession in place of the prime minister, who is approved by parliament.

After polls closed, the Central Electoral Commission (CEC) announced that all 29 amendments were approved by 69.8 percent of registered voters. While observers from the Council of Europe's Parliamentary Assembly reported the referendum was well executed, independent election observers who were unaccredited identified numerous instances of ballot stuffing, carousel voting, and other irregularities, many of which were captured on video. They also observed significantly lower turnout than was officially reported by the CEC.

Political Parties and Political Participation: While there were 50 registered political parties, the ruling Yeni Azerbaijan Party dominated the political system. Domestic observers reported that membership in the ruling party conferred advantages, such as preference for public positions. The Milli Mejlis has not included representatives of the country's main opposition parties since 2010.

Opposition members were more likely than other citizens to experience official harassment and arbitrary arrest and detention. Members of the N!DA youth movement and the Youth Committee of the Popular Front Party were arrested and sentenced to administrative detention after making social media posts critical of the government. Authorities also attempted to smear the Popular Front Party by insinuating that the PFP was connected to extreme Shiism during the prosecution of the party's deputy chairman, Fuad Gahramanli, for his support of the rights of Muslim Unity Movement members. Authorities similarly alleged ties to Sunni Gulenism when they arrested PFP chairman Ali Karimli's assistant, Faig Amirli.

According to domestic NGOs' joint list of political prisoners, several political detainees or prisoners were opposition party or movement members. At least 12 opposition members were considered to be political prisoners, such as REAL movement chairman Ilgar Mammadov, who was convicted in 2015 and sentenced to seven years' imprisonment for allegedly inciting civil unrest (see section 5). At least 10 opposition figures were considered to be political detainees, including Popular Front deputy chairman Fuad Gahramanli, who was detained in December 2015 on charges that appeared connected with his exercise of freedom of expression (see section 2.a.).

Regional party members often had to conceal the purpose of their gatherings and held them in remote locations. Opposition party members reported police often dispersed small gatherings at teahouses and detained participants for questioning. Opposition parties continued to have difficulty renting office space, reportedly because landlords feared official retaliation; some parties operated from their leaders' apartments.

<u>Participation of Women and Minorities</u>: No laws limit the participation of women and members of minorities in the political process, and women and minorities did participate.

Section 4. Corruption and Lack of Transparency in Government

The law provides criminal penalties for conviction of corruption by officials, but the government did not implement the law effectively, and officials often engaged in corrupt practices with impunity. While the government made some progress combatting low-level corruption in provision of government services, high-level corruption remained a problem. Transparency International and other observers described corruption as widespread during the year.

There were continued reports that authorities targeted some whistleblowers seeking to combat government corruption. For example, activists stated former Zardab district prosecutor Rufat Safarov was framed for extortion after speaking out against corruption in the prosecution service. On September 8, he was convicted in the Lankaran Grave Crimes Court and sentenced to nine years in prison. Local NGOs considered him a political prisoner.

<u>Corruption</u>: There continued to be reports that the families of several high-level officials were beneficiaries of monopolies. Authorities initiated some criminal cases related to bribery and other forms of government corruption during the year, although few senior officials were prosecuted.

Following the October 2015 dismissal of the national security minister Eldar Mahmudov and other ministry officials, in December 2016 the Baku Court of Grave Crimes began a criminal trial against several former high-ranking officials of the now defunct National Security Ministry, accusing them of abuse of power, illegal inspection of businesses, extortion, bribery, and blackmail. The case's investigation had led to the removal of officials from other ministries on related charges of corruption, including the former communications minister Ali Abbasov and nine ministry and public telecommunications employees.

There was widespread belief that a bribe could obtain a waiver of the military service obligation, which is universal for men between the ages of 18 and 35. Citizens also reported military personnel could buy assignments to easier military duties for a smaller bribe.

The president and Presidential Administration continued a well-publicized program to decrease corruption at lower levels of public administration. The State Agency for Public Service and Social Innovations (ASAN) service centers functioned as a one-stop location for government services, such as birth certificates and marriage licenses, from nine ministries.

The Prosecutor General's Office includes an Anticorruption Department that took 201 cases involving 313 persons to court during 2016. The department also sought recovery of proceeds from crime, made recommendations, and issued mandatory instructions to eliminate conditions conducive to corruption.

<u>Financial Disclosure</u>: The law requires officials to submit reports on their financial situation, and the electoral code requires all candidates to submit financial statements. The process of submitting reports was complex and nontransparent, with several agencies and bodies designated as recipients, including the Anticorruption Commission, the Milli Mejlis, the Ministry of Justice, and the Central Election Commission, although their monitoring roles were not well understood. The public did not have access to the reports. The law contemplates administrative sanctions for noncompliance, but the sanctions were not imposed.

The law prohibits the public release of the names and capital investments of business owners. Critics claimed the amendments were an attempt to curb investigative journalism into government officials' business interests and could decrease public access to information.

Public Access to Information: The law provides for public access to government information by individuals and organizations, but the government often did not allow it. Various ministries routinely denied requests, claiming not to possess information, although the ministries also claimed to have separate procedures on how to request information. Individuals have the right to appeal denials in court, but the courts generally upheld ministry decisions.

Section 5. Governmental Attitude Regarding International and Nongovernmental Investigation of Alleged Violations of Human Rights

The government continued to limit severely the operations of domestic and international human rights groups during the year. Application of restrictive laws to constrain NGO activities, and other pressure continued at the high level of recent years. Leading human rights NGOs faced a hostile environment for investigating and publishing their findings on human rights cases. As a result, some activists left, others stayed outside the country, and a number of NGOs remained unable to operate. While authorities released at least four human rights defenders, their ability to work was constrained by the overall restrictions on NGO activities. Prominent human rights defender Aliabbas Rustamov remained incarcerated and was widely considered a political prisoner. In addition, authorities imposed restrictions such as travel bans on some of the defenders, including on prominent human rights lawyer Intigam Aliyev, and had not returned Aliyev's case files or his organization's office equipment as of year's end.

While the government maintained ties with some human rights NGOs and responded to their inquiries, on numerous occasions it criticized and intimidated other human rights NGOs and activists. The Ministry of Justice continued to deny registration or placed burdensome administrative restrictions on human rights NGOs on arbitrary grounds. Activists also reported that authorities refused to register their organizations or grants, continued investigations into organizations' activities, froze their personal and organizational bank accounts, and did not return previously seized office equipment. Some NGO representatives also reported that they or a family member suffered physical assault with impunity. Many representatives reported difficulty locating office or event space, particularly in hotels and especially for events occurring outside Baku.

Senior government officials engaged in ad hominem attacks on human rights activists. State-run media outlets accused Amnesty International, Human Rights Watch, Freedom House, and Reporters without Borders of supporting "antinational elements." On multiple occasions, Presidential Administration officials accused local and foreign NGOs of representing foreign interests seeking to destabilize the country and, therefore, of subversive activity, naming specific democracy and human rights groups and activists who had been incarcerated.

During the year a government council provided 5.25 million manat ($2.9 million) to 520 NGOs. While observers considered many of the NGOs to be progovernment or politically neutral, some NGOs that criticized the government also received grants.

<u>The United Nations or Other International Bodies</u>: The government viewed with suspicion statements from such organizations, claiming these international bodies had no right to act in ways authorities saw as interfering in the country's internal affairs.

On September 22, the UN special rapporteur on the situation of human rights defenders, Michel Forst, stated, "civil society of Azerbaijan faces the worst situation since the independence of the country" and called on authorities to rethink their "punitive approach to civil society." He also noted arrests and detentions of individuals prior to a peaceful protest on September 17 as well as administrative and legal pressure being applied to NGOs and called on the government to establish a dialogue with human rights defenders.

Following the government's July 2015 closure of the OSCE's Baku office, the OSCE remained unable to re-establish operations in the country.

<u>Government Human Rights Bodies</u>: Citizens may appeal violations committed by the state or by individuals to the Ombudsman's Office of the Republic of Azerbaijan for human rights, Elmira Suleymanova, or the ombudsman for human rights for the Nakhchivan Autonomous Republic, Ulkar Bayramova. The ombudsman may refuse to accept cases of abuse that are more than a year old, anonymous, or already being handled by the judiciary. Human rights NGOs criticized the Ombudsman's Office as lacking independence and effectiveness in cases considered politically motivated.

The Ombudsman's Office of the Republic of Azerbaijan reported receiving 18,740 complaints in 2016, an increase of 22.3 percent from 2014. The majority of complaints involved alleged violations of property rights, court provisions for the protection of rights and freedoms, social benefits, and labor rights. The Ombudsman's Office reportedly resolved 63.6 percent of complaints accepted for consideration.

The Ombudsman's Office of the Nakhchivan Autonomous Republic reported receiving 37 complaints in 2016. The main subjects of the complaints were on labor and social protection rights. The Ombudsman's Office stated that 10 complaints were resolved successfully and violations of the law were not identified in 27 cases.

Human rights offices in the Milli Mejlis and the Ministry of Justice also heard complaints, conducted investigations, and made recommendations to relevant government bodies.

Section 6. Discrimination, Societal Abuses, and Trafficking in Persons

Women

Rape and Domestic Violence: Rape is illegal and carries a maximum sentence of 15 years in prison. During the year the Ministry of Internal Affairs reported 31 cases of rape and 62 cases of violence of a sexual nature. The ministry stated that 54 persons had been brought to trial for these offenses.

The law establishes a framework for the investigation of domestic violence complaints, defines a process to issue restraining orders, and calls for the establishment of a shelter and rehabilitation center for survivors. Some critics of the domestic violence law asserted that a lack of clear implementing guidelines reduced its effectiveness. Female members of the Milli Mejlis and the head of the State Committee for Family, Women, and Children Affairs (SCFWCA) continued their activities against domestic violence. The committee conducted public awareness campaigns and worked to improve the socioeconomic situation of domestic violence survivors.

Women had limited recourse against assaults by their husbands or others, particularly in rural areas.

The government and an independent NGO each ran a shelter providing assistance and counseling to victims of trafficking and domestic violence.

Sexual Harassment: The government rarely enforced the prohibition of sexual harassment. The SCFWCA worked extensively on women's problems, including organizing and hosting several conferences that raised awareness of sexual harassment and domestic violence.

Reproductive Rights: Couples and individuals have the right to decide the number, spacing, and timing of their children; manage their reproductive health; and had access to the information and means to do so, free from discrimination, coercion, and violence. Contraception was widely available, but demographic surveys showed low levels of use. Patriarchal norms based on cultural, historical, and socioeconomic factors in some cases limited women's reproductive rights.

Discrimination: Although women nominally enjoyed the same legal rights as men, societal discrimination was a problem. Traditional social norms and lagging economic development in rural regions restricted women's roles in the economy, and there were reports women had difficulty exercising their legal rights due to gender discrimination. There was discrimination against women in employment (see section 7.d.). The SCFWCA conducted public-media campaigns to raise awareness of women's rights.

Gender-biased Sex Selection: The gender ratio of children born in the country was 114 boys for 100 girls, according to the UN Population Fund. Local experts reported that gender-biased sex selection was widespread, predominantly in rural regions. The SCFWCA conducted seminars and public media campaigns to raise awareness of the problem.

Children

Birth Registration: Children derive citizenship by birth within the country or from their parents. Registration at birth was routine for births in hospitals or clinics. Some children born at home (for example, to Romani or impoverished families) were not registered, and statelessness for those children was a problem. The Ministries of Internal Affairs and Justice registered undocumented children after identifying them as a population vulnerable to trafficking.

Education: While education was compulsory, free, and universal until the age of 17, large families in impoverished rural areas sometimes placed a higher priority on the education of boys and kept girls in the home to work. Some poor families forced their children to work or beg rather than attend school. Although the country scored well in adult literacy and achieving gender parity indexes in the UNESCO *Education for All Global Monitoring Report*, it fell either "very far from target" or "far from target" in preprimary, primary, and lower secondary education enrollment projections for the year.

<u>Child Abuse</u>: During the year the Ministry of Internal Affairs reported 179 cases of violence against minors, including six cases of rape involving underage victims, 47 cases of minors subjected to sexual acts, and two cases of forced prostitution. According to the ministry, 139 persons were brought to trial in connection with these cases.

<u>Early and Forced Marriage</u>: The law provides that a girl may marry at the age of 18 or at 17 with local authorities' permission. The law further states that a boy may marry at the age of 18. The Caucasus Muslim Board defines 18 as the marriage age, but the fatwa failed to have much effect on religious marriage contracts (kabin or kabin-nama).

The criminal code establishes fines of 3,000 to 4,000 manat ($1,670 to $2,220) or imprisonment of up to four years for conviction of the crime of forced marriage with underage children. According to the UN special rapporteur, in 2014 forced marriages of underage girls remained a problem and continued to endanger their lives. A 2014 UN Population Fund report stated that 12 percent of girls were married by the age of 18.

NGOs reported that the number of early marriages continued to increase. Girls who married under the terms of religious marriage contracts were of particular concern, since these were not subject to government oversight and do not entitle the wife to recognition of her status in case of divorce. The Social Union of Solidarity among Women reported numerous instances in which men moved to Russia for work, leaving their underage wives in the country.

The SCFWCA conducted activities in IDP and refugee communities to prevent early marriage.

<u>Sexual Exploitation of Children</u>: The law prohibits pornography; its production, distribution, or advertisement is punishable by three years' imprisonment. Statutory rape is defined as "the sexual relations or other actions of a sexual nature, committed by a person who has reached 18, with a person who has not reached 16" and is punishable by up to three years' imprisonment. Recruitment of minors for prostitution (involving a minor in immoral acts) is punishable by three to five years

in prison, although the presence of aggravating factors, such as violence, could increase the potential sentence to five to eight years.

A Baku group working with street children reported that boys and girls at times engaged in prostitution and street begging.

Displaced Children: A large number of refugee and internally displaced children lived in substandard conditions. In some cases, these children were unable to attend school.

International Child Abductions: The country is not a party to the 1980 Hague Convention on the Civil Aspects of International Child Abduction. . See the Department of State's *Annual Report on International Parental Child Abduction* at travel.state.gov/content/childabduction/en/legal/compliance.html.

Anti-Semitism

The country's Jewish community was estimated to be between 20,000 and 30,000 individuals. There were no reports of anti-Semitic acts.

Trafficking in Persons

See the Department of State's *Trafficking in Persons Report* at www.state.gov/j/tip/rls/tiprpt/.

Persons with Disabilities

The law prohibits discrimination against persons with physical, sensory, intellectual, and mental disabilities in employment, education, air travel and other transportation, access to health care, or the provision of other state services, but the government did not enforce these provisions effectively. Employment discrimination remained a problem (see section 7.d.).

A common belief persisted that children with disabilities were ill and needed to be separated from other children and institutionalized, but specific educational facilities were available to children with some disabilities, for example, those with vision disabilities. Children with certain disabilities, including autism, received no education benefits or allowances. A local NGO reported there were approximately 60,000 children with disabilities in the country, of whom 6,000 to 10,000 had access to specialized educational facilities, while the rest were educated at home or not at all. The ability of children with disabilities to attend school was based on several factors, such as an evaluation by a medical committee, the type of disability, and the resources and physical structure of the family and the desired school. No laws mandate access to public or other buildings, information, or communications for persons with disabilities, and most buildings were not accessible.

Conditions in facilities for persons with mental and other disabilities varied. Qualified staff, equipment, and supplies at times were lacking.

The Ministries of Health and of Labor and Social Welfare are responsible for protecting the rights of persons with disabilities.

National/Racial/Ethnic Minorities

Citizens of Armenian descent reported discrimination in employment (see section 7.d.). Some groups reported sporadic incidents of discrimination, restrictions on their ability to teach in their native languages, and harassment by local authorities. These groups included Talysh in the south, Lezghi in the north, and Meskhetians and Kurds.

Acts of Violence, Discrimination, and Other Abuses Based on Sexual Orientation and Gender Identity

Antidiscrimination laws exist but do not specifically cover lesbian, gay, bisexual, transgender, and intersex (LGBTI) individuals.

Societal intolerance, violence, and discrimination based on sexual orientation and gender identity remained a problem. A local NGO reported that there were numerous incidents of police brutality against individuals based on sexual orientation and noted that authorities did not investigate or punish those responsible. There were also reports of family-based violence against LGBTI individuals and hostile Facebook postings on personal online accounts. A local organization reported that in the first eight months of the year, one gay and two transgender persons were killed and one transvestite committed suicide. In October media reported an attack on a group of LGBTI persons in the Baku City metro.

LGBTI individuals refused to file formal complaints of discrimination or mistreatment with law enforcement bodies due to fear of social stigma or retaliation. An NGO reported police indifference to investigating crimes committed against the LGBTI community.

There was societal prejudice and employment discrimination (see section 7.d.) against LGBTI persons.

HIV and AIDS Social Stigma

In the country's most recent demographic and health survey (2006), 80 percent of women and 92 percent of men reported discriminatory attitudes towards persons with HIV. The World Health Organization's *Review of the HIV Program in Azerbaijan* (2014) noted that discriminatory attitudes and overall lack of information about HIV/AIDS remained high. The issue was addressed in the *Azerbaijan National Strategic Plan for HIV 2016-2020*.

Section 7. Worker Rights

a. Freedom of Association and the Right to Collective Bargaining

The law provides for freedom of association, including the right to form and join independent labor unions. Uniformed military and police and managerial staff are prohibited from joining unions. While the law provides workers the right to bargain collectively, unions could not effectively negotiate wage levels and working conditions because government-appointed boards ran major state-owned firms and set wages for government employees.

The law provides most workers the right to conduct legal strikes. Categories of workers prohibited from striking include high-ranking executive and legislative officials; law enforcement officers; court employees; fire fighters; and health, electric power, water supply, telephone, railroad, and air traffic control workers.

The law prohibits discrimination against trade unions and labor activists and requires the reinstatement of workers fired for union activity. The law also prohibits retribution against strikers, such as dismissal or replacement. Striking workers who disrupt public transportation, however, could be sentenced to up to three years in prison.

The Azerbaijan Trade Unions Confederation (ATUC) was the only trade union confederation in the country. The trade union registration process was cumbersome and time consuming. Although ATUC registered as an independent organization, some workers considered it closely aligned with the government. ATUC reported that it represented 1.6 million members in 27 sectors at the start of the year. Regardless of whether a company was a member of ATUC, a labor inspector appointed under the Ministry of Labor and Social Protection could investigate labor-related grievances.

The government did not effectively enforce laws regarding freedom of association and collective bargaining. Administrative penalties were not sufficient to deter violations. Administrative and judicial procedures were subject to lengthy delays and appeals. There were some restrictions, such as increased bureaucratic scrutiny on the right to form unions and conduct union activities. Most unions were not independent, and the overwhelming majority remained tightly linked to the government, with the exception of some journalists' unions. Both local and international NGOs claimed that workers in most industries were largely unaware of their rights and afraid of retribution if they initiated complaints. This was especially true for workers in the public sector.

Collective bargaining agreements were often treated as formalities and not enforced. Although the labor law applies to all workers and enterprises, the government may negotiate bilateral agreements that effectively exempt multi-national enterprises from it. For example, production-sharing agreements between the government and multi-national energy enterprises did not provide for employee participation in a trade union. While the law prohibits employers from impeding the collective bargaining process, employers engaged in activities that undercut the effectiveness of collective bargaining, such as subcontracting and using short-term employment agreements.

The state oil company's 65,200 workers were required to belong to the Union of Oil and Gas Industry Workers, and authorities automatically deducted union dues (2 percent of each worker's salary) from paychecks. Many of the state-owned enterprises that dominated the formal economy withheld union dues from workers' pay but did not deliver the dues to the unions. Employers officially withheld a quarter of the dues collected for the oil workers' union for "administrative costs" associated with running the union. A complete lack of transparency made it impossible to determine exactly how the union spent the dues. Unions and their members had no means of investigating the matter.

On April 2, a group of laborers of the Baku-based Azimport company protested the nonpayment of salaries. Protesters reported that the company employed them for more than a year to overhaul buildings and facilities in the city and failed to pay salaries. Sporadic complaints of nonpayment of salaries often became impromptu small-scale protests throughout the country. For example, employees of Azerinsaatservis LLC frequently complained to media about nonpayment of salaries.

b. Prohibition of Forced or Compulsory Labor

The law prohibits all forms of forced or compulsory labor, except in circumstances of war or in the execution of a court decision under the supervision of a government agency. The government did not effectively enforce applicable laws. Resources and inspections were inadequate. Penalties for violations, including imprisonment, were generally sufficient to deter violations. A report of the International Labor Organization on the application of international labor standards urged the government to stop the use of compulsory labor as punishment against those expressing their political or ideological views.

During the year authorities directed many government employees outside of the capital to participate in the autumn cotton harvest. Migrant workers were at times subjected to conditions of forced labor in the construction industry. Forced begging by children was a problem, and domestic servitude was an emerging problem. Men and boys at times were subjected to conditions of forced labor within the country, for example, in construction (see section 7.c.). The Ministry of Internal Affairs reported that it identified five cases of forced labor in the first nine months of the year. During the year the antitrafficking department in the Ministry of Internal Affairs inspected construction and agricultural sector sites but did not identify any victims of labor trafficking.

Also see the Department of State's *Trafficking in Persons Report* at www.state.gov/j/tip/rls/tiprpt/.

c. Prohibition of Child Labor and Minimum Age for Employment

The minimum age for employment depends on the type of work. In most cases the law permits children to work from the age of 15; children who are 14 may work in family businesses or, with parental consent, in daytime after-school jobs that pose no hazard to their health. Children under the age of 16 may not work more than 24 hours per week; children who are 16 or 17 may not work more than 36 hours per week. The law prohibits employing children under the age of 18 in difficult and hazardous conditions and identifies specific work and industries in which children are prohibited, including work with toxic substances and underground, at night, in mines, and in nightclubs, bars, casinos, or other businesses that serve alcohol.

The Ministry of Labor and Social Security is responsible for enforcing child labor laws. The law provides for a fine or imprisonment as punishment for employing individuals without an effective employment agreement, providing protection to children working without a contract. The SCFWCA trained regional Labor Inspection Service representatives, police inspectors, and local authorities in preventing child labor exploitation. Several labor NGOs not designated as labor organizations focused on child labor in the industrial and agricultural sectors.

Government enforcement of the laws prohibiting child labor and setting a minimum age for employment was inconsistent. Resources and inspections were inadequate and penalties for violations, including fines, did not always deter violations. Although the ministry conducted inspections during the year, a local NGO reported there was a need for increased monitoring.

There were few complaints of abuses of child labor laws during the year, although there were anecdotal reports of child labor in agriculture, forced begging, and street work and that children were subjected to commercial sexual exploitation (see section 6, Children).

Also see the Department of Labor's *Findings on the Worst Forms of Child Labor* at www.dol.gov/ilab/reports/child-labor/findings/.

d. Discrimination with Respect to Employment and Occupation

The labor code prohibits discrimination with respect to employment and occupation on the basis of citizenship, race, color, sex, religion, political opinion, national origin or citizenship, social origin, disability, sexual orientation or gender identity, age, language, affiliation with trade unions or other public associations, or professional standing. The law does not specifically prohibit discrimination based on HIV-positive status or other communicable diseases, but there were no media or NGO reports of such discrimination. The government did not always enforce these laws effectively, and employment discrimination remained a problem.

Individuals under the implied protection of law against discrimination reported the law was not applied. Employers generally hesitated to hire persons with disabilities; citizens of Armenian descent reported discrimination in employment as well. Discrimination in employment and occupation also occurred with respect to sexual orientation. LGBTI individuals reported employers found other reasons to dismiss them because they could not legally dismiss someone because of their sexual orientation.

The law excludes women from certain occupations with inherently dangerous conditions, such as working underground in mines. Women were underrepresented in high-level jobs, including top business positions. Traditional practices limited women's access to economic opportunities in rural areas.

e. Acceptable Conditions of Work

As of August 21, the national minimum wage was 105 manat ($58) per month. The average poverty line was 136 manat ($76) per month, with 146 manat ($81) the poverty level for able-bodied persons, 115 manat ($64) for pensioners, and 117 manat ($65) for children. The law requires equal pay for equal work regardless of gender, age, or other classification.

The law provides for a 40-hour workweek; the maximum daily work shift is 12 hours. Workers in hazardous occupations may not work more than 36 hours per week. The law requires lunch and rest periods that are determined by labor contracts and collective agreements. Information was not available on whether local companies provided the legally required premium compensation for overtime, although international companies generally did. There is no prohibition on excessive compulsory overtime. The law provides equal rights to foreign and domestic workers.

Ministry of Labor and ATUC officials inspected worksites for compliance, particularly in the construction, energy, and oil sectors, and recommended improvements in labor conditions to employers. Most individuals worked part time in the informal sector (unregistered businesses), which accounted for between 10 and 30 percent of the economy, and where the government did not enforce contracts or labor laws.

The government did not effectively enforce the laws on acceptable conditions of work. Local human rights groups, including the Oil Workers Rights Defense Council, an NGO dedicated to protecting worker rights in the petroleum sector, maintained that employers, particularly foreign oil companies, did not always treat foreign and domestic workers equally. Domestic employees of foreign oil companies reportedly often received lower pay and worked without contracts or health care. Some domestic employees of foreign oil companies reported violations of the national labor code, noting they were unable to receive overtime payments or vacations.

Inspection of working conditions by the Ministry of Labor and Social Protection's labor inspectorate was weak and ineffective. The ministry's 267 labor inspectors were insufficient to monitor worksites, and penalties for violations were seldom enforced. Although the law sets health and safety standards, employers widely ignored them. Violations of acceptable conditions of work in the construction and oil and gas sectors remained problematic. In December 2015 a total of 31 oil workers died in a Caspian Sea deep-water oil rig fire started by a gas pipeline explosion that burned for several weeks. The Prosecutor General's Office opened a criminal case but did not release its findings to the public. The Oil Workers Rights Protection Organization (OWRPO) reported that the state oil company managers broke safety laws for the sake of continuing production and that workers did not have life jackets when they attempted to evacuate the platform. Families of missing oil workers complained about mistreatment by state officials when they tried to obtain information following the accident. A special commission led by Prime Minister Artur Rasizade was tasked to investigate the incident. The commission's report was presented to the Presidential Administration but not made public.

On December 15, strong winds destroyed part of pier related to oil operations, resulting in the death of 10 workers. The OWRPO stated the infrastructure was old and had not been properly maintained.

During the year there were reports of Azerbaijan Airlines workers forced to work longer hours for less pay. There were also reports that senior executives required airline crews to forgo hotel rooms for rest and instead remain onboard their planes.

ATUC reported good cooperation with Russian and Georgian authorities on measures to protect Russian and Georgian migrant workers' rights and the safety of working conditions. The Ministries of Labor and Internal Affairs reportedly monitored the labor rights of other workers in hazardous sectors and in the informal economy. Workers may remove themselves from situations that endanger health or safety, but there is no legal protection of their employment if they did so.